T0413472

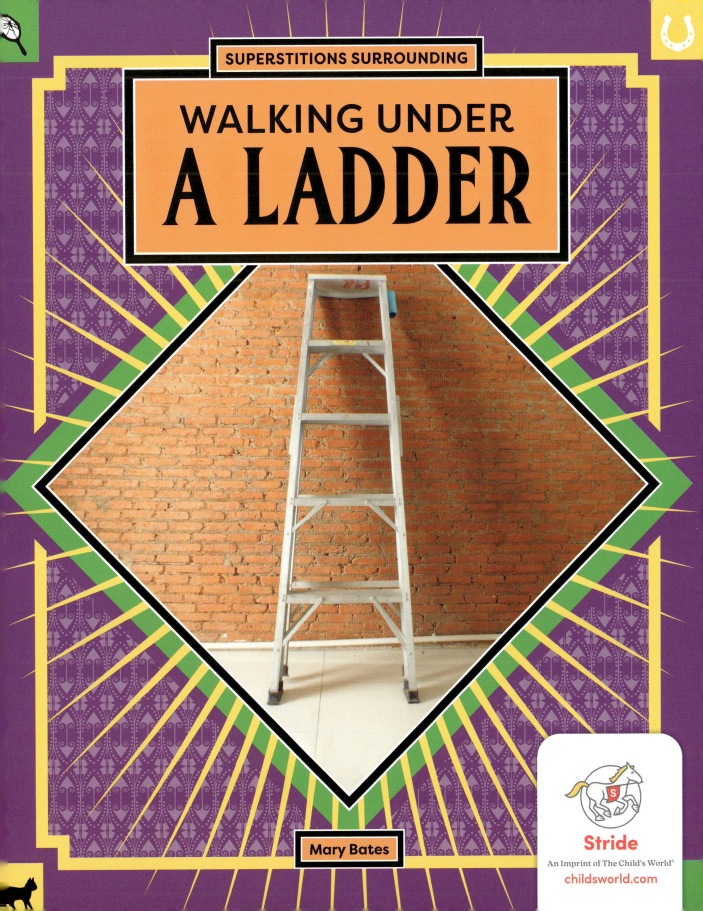

**Published by The Child's World®**
800-599-READ • childsworld.com

**Copyright © 2023 by The Child's World®**
All rights reserved. No part of this book may be reproduced or utilized in any form or by any means without written permission from the publisher.

**Photography Credits**
Photographs ©: Tus Bom/Shutterstock Images, cover, 1; George Green/Shutterstock Images, 5; Sorapop Udomsri/Shutterstock Images, 7; Shutterstock Images, 8, 17, 18, 21; Everett Collection/Shutterstock Images, 9; iStockphoto, 11, 12, 15; Jaroslav Moravcik/Shutterstock Images, 13

**ISBN Information**
9781503865051 (Reinforced Library Binding)
9781503866492 (Portable Document Format)
9781503867338 (Online Multi-user eBook)
9781503868175 (Electronic Publication)

**LCCN** 2022939493

**Printed in the United States of America**

**About the Author**
Mary Bates is a freelance science writer and author. She specializes in writing about the brains and behaviors of humans and other animals for curious audiences of all ages. Her work has appeared in numerous print and online publications.

CHAPTER ONE
**Unlucky Ladders. . . 4**

CHAPTER TWO
**Origins . . . 10**

CHAPTER THREE
**Walking Under a Ladder Today . . . 16**

Glossary . . . 22

Fast Facts . . . 23

One Stride Further . . . 23

Find Out More . . . 24

Index . . . 24

CHAPTER ONE

# UNLUCKY LADDERS

When a ladder is leaning against the side of a building, it leaves a space between the building and the ladder. This space is often big enough for a person to walk through, but people usually avoid it. That is because walking under a ladder is supposed to bring bad luck.

This is an example of a superstition. A superstition is a belief that an action can bring good or bad luck. There is no **logical** reason for the belief. However, many people believe in superstitions.

*Many people believe that walking under a ladder is bad luck.*

If someone does walk under a ladder, there are supposedly a few ways to reverse the bad luck. Some people believe a person should cross her fingers and keep them crossed until she sees a dog. Others say people should walk backward under the ladder. Some people believe a person will not have bad luck if he makes a wish while walking under the ladder.

In 2019, researchers talked to 1,220 U.S. adults. Twenty-one percent said they believed that walking under a ladder brings bad luck.

*Some superstitions, like crossing fingers, are believed to offer protection against bad luck.*

Superstitions like this one did not just appear out of nowhere. The ladder superstition goes back thousands of years. People in different cultures have different reasons to avoid walking under ladders. Most of the reasons involve more magic than logic. But this superstition may also be based on common sense.

*Even people who do not believe in superstitions try not to walk under ladders. That is because it is unsafe!*

CHAPTER TWO

# ORIGINS

Many superstitious beliefs began a long time ago. That is why it is difficult to pin down the sources of most superstitions. However, it is believed the superstition of bad luck from walking under a ladder began 5,000 years ago in ancient Egypt.

**The oldest known cave paintings include images of ladderlike shapes. They were created in Spain by Neanderthals—early relatives of modern humans—at least 64,000 years ago.**

*The superstition of walking under a ladder may have started in ancient Egypt.*

*The ancient Egyptians believed that pyramids were ladders to heaven.*

When a ladder leans against a wall, it forms a triangle shape with the wall and the ground. Triangles were **sacred** to the ancient Egyptians. Examples of sacred triangles are the pyramids the Egyptians built for their kings, or pharaohs. People may have believed that passing through a triangle created by a resting ladder would break its sacred power.

The number three is significant to Christians, too. It reflects the Holy Trinity. The Trinity is a reflection of God, Jesus, and the Holy Spirit. Since a triangle has three sides, it often **symbolizes** the Trinity. Early Christians may have thought that walking under the triangle of a ladder was disrespectful to their God.

Ladders were linked to death in the Middle Ages (500–1500 AD). In Europe, ladders were often associated with **gallows**. If someone walked under a ladder, it was said that he or she would eventually die by hanging. There is an even more recent connection between ladders, gallows, and misfortune. Criminals in the 1600s in England often walked under a ladder on their way to the gallows to face their death.

*Public executions of criminals used to be open for people to observe.*

CHAPTER THREE

# WALKING UNDER A LADDER TODAY

One reason people avoid walking under ladders is because it could be dangerous. If a ladder is resting against a wall, there could be someone on it. There is a chance that something could fall on a passerby's head if he or she walks under the ladder.

In 2005, the Handwerks Museum in Austria made the longest ladder in the world. The wooden ladder has 120 **rungs** and is 135 feet (41 m) long.

*Walking under a ladder can be dangerous, especially if someone is on it.*

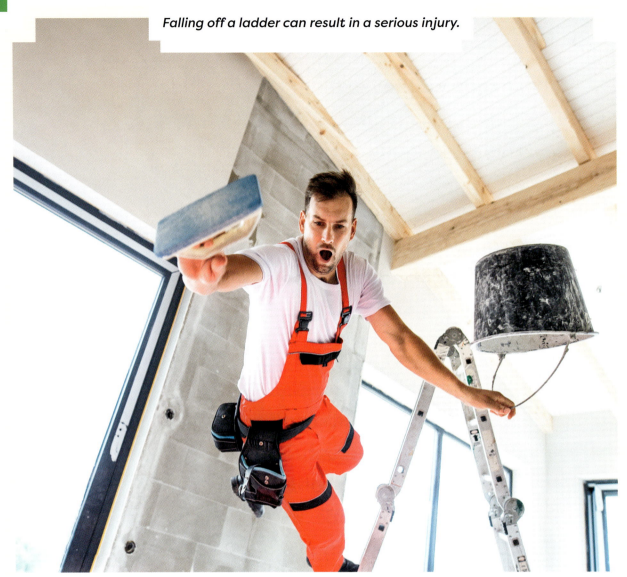

*Falling off a ladder can result in a serious injury.*

Also, people should be careful around ladders for the safety of those working on them. A person could accidentally bump into a ladder and knock someone down. That is why it is better to walk around a ladder rather than under it.

These reasons may explain why the superstition around ladders started and stuck around.

There are many different superstitions. That is because people make **correlations** between two events that are not actually related. For instance, a person walks under a ladder. Soon after, he or she might trip and fall. People who believe in the ladder superstition might say the bad luck from walking under the ladder caused the fall.

Each year in the United States, more than 300,000 people are treated for ladder-related injuries. Since 2017, people have observed National Ladder Safety Month in March. The purpose of National Ladder Safety Month is to raise awareness of ladder safety and decrease the number of ladder-related injuries.

Some people think that a belief in superstitions is **irrational**. But there are still a lot of people who hold these beliefs. That is because believing in superstitions can help manage stressful feelings that come from not knowing what is going to happen in the future. For many people, these beliefs provide a sense of control and reduce **anxiety**.

Finally, even if people do not fully believe in a superstition, they may still follow it. They may not want to take a chance that the superstition is true. And there is little to lose by not walking under ladders. In fact, it is safer for both the person walking and the individual on the rungs of the ladder. For some people, this is reason enough. For others, the superstition about bad luck is what makes them avoid walking under ladders.

*Even though science considers superstitious beliefs to be false, many people still believe in them to give them comfort.*

# GLOSSARY

**anxiety** (ang-ZY-uh-tee) Anxiety is a feeling of fear or nervousness about what might happen. Belief in superstitions may help soothe a person's anxiety.

**correlations** (kor-uh-LAY-shunz) Connections between two or more things are known as correlations. People often make correlations between events that occur close together in time.

**gallows** (GAL-ohz) Gallows are structures from which criminals are hanged. Since ladders are sometimes linked to the gallows, ladders are associated with misfortune and death.

**irrational** (eer-RASH-uh-null) If something is not based on reason, it is irrational. Superstitions are sometimes irrational, yet many people still believe in them.

**logical** (LAH-jik-ull) Something that is logical has clear reason. A logical person will tend to believe in science over superstition.

**rungs** (RUHNGZ) Rungs are the horizontal bars of a ladder. People use rungs to support their feet as they go up ladders.

**sacred** (SAY-krid) Something that is holy or connected to religion is considered sacred. Egyptians believed that triangles were sacred.

**symbolizes** (SIM-buh-lize-uhz) A design or object that stands for something else symbolizes that idea. The triangle symbolizes the Christian trinity.

# FAST FACTS

- Some people believe in the superstition that walking under a ladder will bring a person bad luck.

- This superstition started in ancient Egypt. The triangular shape made by a resting ladder was considered sacred.

- Ladders have been associated with gallows for centuries, so ladders are seen as symbols of death and misfortune.

- It is safer to avoid walking under ladders.

# ONE STRIDE FURTHER

- Why might more people believe in superstitions during stressful or uncertain times? How do you think superstitious beliefs might help people?

- Do you believe in any superstitions? Does anyone in your family? How do you think family members influence someone's belief in superstitions?

# FIND OUT MORE

### IN THE LIBRARY
Dalgleish, Sharon. *Crossing Your Fingers.*
Parker, CO: The Child's World, 2023.

Johnson, C. M. *Superstitions.* Minneapolis, MN: Lerner, 2018.

Newland, Sonya. *The Genius of the Ancient Egyptians.* New York, NY: Crabtree, 2020.

### ON THE WEB
Visit our website for links about walking under a ladder:
**childsworld.com/links**

*Note to Parents, Teachers, and Librarians: We routinely verify our Web links to make sure they are safe and active sites. So encourage your readers to check them out!*

# INDEX

ancient Egypt, 10–13

cave paintings, 10
Christians, 14

gallows, 14

injuries, 16–19

Middle Ages, 14

National Ladder Safety Month, 19

pyramids, 13

reverse bad luck, 6
rungs, 16, 20

safety, 16–19, 20